Journey For God's Purpose

"An Impossible Journey
Meant For Good"

By

AC Williams

Journey For God's Purpose

"An Impossible Journey Meant For Good"

By:

AC Williams

Published By:

ABM Publications
A division of Andrew Bills Ministries, Inc.
PO Box 6811, Orange, CA 92863
www.abmpublications.com

ISBN: 978-1-931820-30-1

PRAISE AND THANKS TO GOD

All glory to you Father in Heaven
for blessing me with this opportunity to serve you.

I Love You!

AC WILLIAMS

ACKNOWLEDGEMENTS

To My Daughter, Kaelin William-Bone,
All I Needed You To Be;
Patient and Helpful

To My Daughter, Bre William-Klein
All You Were To Me;
Supportive And Encouraging

To My Granddaughter, Bailee Monroe
For All You Are Becoming.

To My Best Friend, Isabel Solomon
For All You Were To Me;
My Rock Of Inspiration.

To My Niece, Colleen Williams
For Your Patience And Support From Day One,
True Heart For Family.

To Murphy Benard,
For Your Unforgettable Love

My Brother, Phillip McGlothin
For all Your Wisdom and Support

And To all Others,
Thank You!

ENDORSEMENTS

I highly recommend you take a look at AC Williams' journey through her physical, emotional and spiritual struggles as she guides you though the process of developing a healthy lifestyle when you place your life in the hands of the Most High God. This story will inspire you and I pray that it will bless you to a point where you, too can share her story with those who are experiencing these same difficulties and yet can become victorious in spite of them. God Bless!

Lynn Williams
Author & Publisher for Royal candlelight Christian Publishing Company

AC Williams tells an inspiring story of how she survived childhood abuse and cancer, how she grew up in a Muslim household and finally found her own path to God as an adult. AC is a survivor whose story has life lessons for all of us. She will make you cry, make you laugh and inspire you to live the greatness within you.

Lee Pound
The Write Coach, Editor and Book Publisher

We had the privilege of having AC Williams as a guest speaker for our LifeStream Singles Ministry at Water of Life Community church. She did an excellent job of communicating her journey in life and how her faith has allowed her to overcome various trials in her life. I believe she was able to inspire the people in our group through her testimony as well as encourage them to continue trusting God even in the midst of difficult circumstances.

Chuck Belk
Singles Pastor – Water of Life Community Church

II Corinthians 5:17 says, "If any man be in Christ, he is a new creature, old things are passed away, behold all things are become new." No matter what a person has previously experienced, we must not allow our past to enslave us to negative thoughts, unforgiveness, ungodly enticements or destructive allurements. AC Williams' testimony exemplifies this. Her story reveals that our past sorrows can become our strong points as we turn to Christ and live in the power of The Holy Spirit of God. Her book has been published as an encouragement to demonstrate that through faith in God, you can arise from a wounded past and walk in the victory that Christ Jesus has given us.

Andrew Bills
Pastor/Evangelist of The Victory Report Hour International Ministries and the president of ABM Publications.

TABLE OF CONTENTS

PREFACE

I have written this book for those
who are in search of positive change,
a path to God and His purpose for their life.

MY MISSION IS:
To inspire people to embrace their journey and
bring awareness of purpose.

May *"JOURNEY FOR GOD'S PURPOSE"* be
a source of great inspiration to
those who came before me,
those who are here and
those who are yet to come.

Thank You,

AC WILLIAMS

INTRODUCTION

My name is AC Williams. I am a survivor of child abuse and (multiple Myeloma) cancer. I believe I was chosen to go through this journey so that I could share with the world just how wonderful God is and how much He wants a relationship with us to build our trust for a holy life.

I'm blessed to touch lives with my story and give hope to those who are in search of a path to God so they can pursue their happiness abundantly.

My aspiration is for you to have a personal relationship with God so you can experience all the wonderful plans for your life, as you cope with your struggles and overcome your adversity through hope and faith. It's to help encourage you with love so you can pursue your purpose in life.

Through building a deep and personal relationship with God, it helped me to surrender my life and it helped me trust in God despite of what I was going through. I decided I was not going to be a victim, that I was going to take life one day at a time, knowing God will give me the strength and courage to get through my situation and anything that comes my way.

I hope that my story and how I was able to deal with my shortcomings through the power of faith will help you with your challenges to find your purpose and share your story.

Go through your journey and use it as a lesson, knowing God is preparing you for something bigger than yourself to share with the world.

Pursue your relationship with God and He will give to you the things you are called to do. When your story gives hope, your life has meaning.

Let the journey begin, God bless.

Chapter 1

The Good Life As A Young Child

I remember living in San Francisco for a few years with my mom, dad and seven siblings. I'm from a family of thirteen, nine sisters and four brothers. I'm the eleventh child born. Most of my brothers and sisters were a lot older and had already moved out of the house.

I was very young, maybe about six when we lived in San Francisco. I remember my mom and dad having a pretty good relationship with each other. It was nice, we were a family. My mom stayed home and took care of us and my dad worked in construction. My dad provided a nice comfortable home for us to live in. It was a nice, stable environment and we were a close family. I felt so much love and security around me.

I really enjoyed my sisters because we did everything together. We would make up games to play and share our toys with each other. My mom and dad had a lot of love for each other and they gave us a lot of love too. It was nice having both my parents around. My mom was always home taking care of whatever we needed which made me happy. I never heard my parents argue.

One of my best memories about San Francisco was our Sunday Family dinners. I enjoyed my mom's cooking because she cooked everything from scratch. She put a lot of love in our meals. When she made homemade cornbread, "which was sweet like a cake," she would let me or one of my sisters lick the bowl before she washed the dishes. I remember it was Sunday because the house would always smell good, like soul food on a holiday.

We had a neighbor that live upstairs who always baked us an apple or pumpkin pie for dessert. Our job, after mom cooked, was to help her set the table and then we would all sit down to eat. We shared a lot of quality time and good memories together at the table. We laughed and clowned around a lot about silly things. When dinner was finished, we cleared the kitchen, then we would sit in the living room and watch a good family movie together.

My mom always planned a picnic in the backyard for us on sunny days. She would gather everything she needed for the blanket and spread it out on the grass and call us outside to eat. We had a nice backyard with the beautiful green grass. It was private, no neighbors could see over the fence and we had a nice mountain view. I loved sitting in the grass. Life was really good for me and my sisters! Those were really happy times for me which lasted for a while.

This was my only memory of us having two parents in the home.

Chapter 2

Abandoned, Scared And Afraid

My parents' relationship started changing. I noticed after awhile, some tension with my parents because my mother started taking trips to Los Angeles on a regular basis and left us with my dad for days at a time. Before this happened, I never heard my parents argue or talk loud for us to hear. I did not understand why my mom was leaving so much. I did not know why at the time, but I found out later, she was going back and forth to Los Angeles to find us a place to live and that came as a shock to me and my sisters.

I did not understand why we had to leave our home because we had a great life. I didn't understand why dad was staying in San Francisco by himself and letting us leave. I was so sad and confused. I later found out mom didn't want to lose the county money she was receiving for us and she did not want to get married. My dad wanted to marry my mom but she was content just being with him. She loved him but not enough to marry him and let him take care of us.

She had a fear of being hurt and abandoned among other reasons. After the constant pressure from my dad to marry him, that's when she decided we were moving to Los Angeles. She wanted my dad just to love her, but he didn't understand why and she didn't tell him.

Dad was so upset with mom, that's when things around the house changed. They started arguing a lot. We didn't spend time eating together any more, no Sunday dinners, no family gatherings in front of the TV, and picnics in the backyard were history.

The good life went out the window and the drama began.

Chapter 3

The Physical Abuse And Anger From My Mom

When we moved back to Los Angeles, things definitely changed around the house, too. We moved in our new place which was a very small apartment with only two bedrooms so some of us had to sleep on the floor. We also had to share one bathroom with eight people in the house that was hard. Right away, mom found a nursing job and started working a lot.

The memories from my mom's childhood started coming back and she began to re-live her past all over again taking her anger out on us. She had a hard exterior and kept her emotions inside, so we didn't get a lot of affection.

Mom always seemed angry and frustrated, I guess she realized now all the responsibilities for taking care of us were on her since dad wasn't around. I began to pick up some of her anger because I was mad at her, so I took it out on my sisters. I noticed we all became more distant with each other due to the absence of our parents not at home to love and nurture us like they used to. A few months passed, out of nowhere my mom decided to join the nation of Islam and enroll us in the Islamic school. I guess she thought Islam would help our situation.

She became angry all the time. She would take her problems out on us. When she spoke, it was like being in military because the tone in her voice was harsh. She was so demanding and angry, when she needed us to do something, like chores, she didn't ask us to do it, she told us in a threatening way. The religion changed her a lot.

My sisters and I were afraid of her because she had a crazy look on her face, like she enjoyed who she was becoming. She seemed to be more concerned about being a Muslim and studying their beliefs than being a mother to us. I became more distant and I did not like being around her so I stayed away as much as possible.

I started wetting the bed because she made me very nervous and I would get beat for that. I tried not to go to sleep because I knew I would wet the bed, but I couldn't stay awake.

We were living in Los Angeles for about a year before the beating got worse. I remember so many times we would get beatings with extension cords, belt buckles, water hoses, wet towels and braided switches.

She would get so angry sometimes, she would put the belt down and start choking and hitting us with her fist. She didn't need a reason to beat us. She would just beat us over any small thing that didn't make sense. A missing cookie from the package or having shoes out of order in the closet even resulted in us being beaten.

I think mom would stage things so she would have a reason to wake us up at 3 AM in the morning and beat us. She would have us line up, then she would talk to us for an hour about something missing in the refrigerator. She would say things like, "I'm gonna give you something to take to your grave." She would beat us one at a time, making us bleed.

The beatings would go on sometimes until the morning just before we had to go to school. Mom got so upset one day when she was whipping my sister, she broke my sister's arm after twisting it. She had to take her to the hospital to get a cast put on it. My sister had to wear a cast for six months and nobody ever asked how it happened.

Another time, she broke my sister's collar bone and made another sister sit on a hot heater. Then another sister, she made hang from a window ledge, trying to make her fall. She beat me with a fireplace tool and she stuffed me in a hot closet for two hours, where I struggled to breathe.

It got so bad, we wanted to do something to hurt my mom. We would think of ways to hurt her, but we didn't do it because we didn't want to go to jail. We would beg and plead with her to stop hurting us, but it didn't help.

There were times mom would wait until we got in the tub and remind us we had a beating coming from something we did days ago. She would wait until we went to bed, then come into our room, ease the blanket off of us, then go crazy with the extension cord, as she'd watch us fall out of bed onto the floor.

My mom would have a smirk on her face as if she was enjoying it. I just felt she used her power to really scare us. I hated to see her beat my sisters and I couldn't do anything to help them. She would beat three of my sisters until she got tired. I don't know if the religion changed her or leaving my dad did it. I just know, she changed from being a loving mom to being a child abuser.

I remember when I was about eleven, I asked my Grandmother Totsie about my mom Sarah's childhood. I wanted to understand why my mom was so angry and abusive to us after we left San Francisco, California. I asked Grandma Totsie, "Did you beat and abuse my mom growing up? It's hard to believe mom's anger came just after we moved to Los Angeles, California."

My Grandma Totsie said, "No, I did not beat Sarah! I did discipline Sarah because she did not want to obey me. Sarah figured since I wasn't her biological mom, she did not have to listen to me. Sarah's anger came from not knowing her biological mom."

Grandma Totsie told my mom Sarah, when she was a teenager, about her past. From that point, mom was rebellious, getting in trouble at school and with her cousins. She rebelled and felt disconnected. I knew it bothered her that we did not look alike, which made it hard for her to open up to me.

Sarah's birth mother was an exchange student from Ethiopia. She came to the United States for a year to study English and got pregnant while she was here. She could not take the baby back home because it would be a disgrace to her family. My Grandma Totsie informed us that her very own husband, which was the biological dad, cheated on her with this exchange student and brought the child home and asked her to help him raise her.

My Grandmother Totsie said, "You can only imagine how I felt, knowing I could not have children, being put in a situation where it's my only way of having a child of my own. I was hurt and angry, but I took on the responsibility and I never took it out on Sarah. Her resentment came from not knowing who she was. Sarah was the daughter I never had, but she wanted to know her real birth mom. It never happened and she carried that pain throughout her life and became bitter."

I felt so alone, sad and unloved.

Chapter 4

The Muslim School

We attended the Islamic Muslim school for years. The school was from first to twelfth grade. I hated that religion because I didn't understand their thinking or what they stood for. I remembered the mean teachers, the unfair education and the overcrowded classrooms with no air conditioners.

I remember being in one classroom for three years during my middle school years and doing the same work. What I noticed during my years as a Muslim was a lot of angry people around me.

Many times I asked myself, "What kind of teachers are running this school, where is the fun and why is mom sending us to this crazy disciplinary school?" We went year round, four days a week, four hours a day and were off on Tuesdays. We had to stay covered up in Muslim uniforms from head to toe year round and there was no playtime. They only believed in study time, religion and discipline. They enforced punishment when anyone got out of line or got bad grades.

The teachers would use a ruler or paddle to swat our hands as punishment. I dreaded every day, getting dressed and walking to school. My sisters and I had to walk past a junior high school in our uniforms and kids would make fun of us as we passed. They would throw rocks at us, so we had to run to and from school which made me uncomfortable and embarrassed.

My sisters and I would take an extra pair of clothes in our bags and walk through the alleys and change so we could get to school safe. Then we would change back again before we got to school. Then we would do the same thing on our way back home. Private school was like living as a nun, sheltered in a hole.

Then Mom took us out of the Muslim school and put us in a public school. It was even more difficult. People knew we came from an all girls' private school so they teased and made fun of us for being a Muslim. It was so hard adjusting to a big school, more kids and more classrooms. We struggled trying to keep up and it was a challenge. We got behind and my mom didn't seem to care. As years passed, my sisters started dropping out of school, but I stayed and finished my education.

Those years were times of great peer pressure, insecurity and low self esteem.

Chapter 5

Latch Key Kids

Mom wasn't at home a lot to see us when we got home from school. We had to let ourselves in the house and rely on each other for the help with homework and getting meals ready.

She had to work, so I held on to my sisters growing up as a teenager because I was the quiet one in the bunch. I leaned on my sisters a lot to help me in areas I was struggling with. I followed my two older sisters a lot of the time and did whatever they would do, just to be around them.

My mom would get angry about every little thing and take it out on us. I don't remember having any happy moments after we left San Francisco. I was still wetting the bed and got more and more beatings for that.

I was very nervous and totally afraid of my mother, so I started running away from home when I was just 13 years old to get away from her abusive behavior.

Finally, I went to live with my dad.

I was feeling lost and extremely sad.

Chapter 6

From The Frying Pan Into The Fire

My dad moved back to Los Angeles two years after we had left San Francisco. He was still very angry with my mom, so we didn't see him much, only on Sundays.

Eventually, I moved in with dad and stayed for two years because I got tired of my mom beating me. My grandparents lived in the house, but I felt like a stranger around them and my dad because it had been two years since I'd seen them.

My dad seemed different because he now had a girlfriend that was half his age. Soon, I noticed when I was around him, his affection towards me became less fatherly and more lustful.

He would say things like, "Come, give daddy some sugar," and he would try to kiss me in the mouth. He would make sexual remarks like, "I see you filling out them pants, girl they look good on you and you're getting kind of thick..."

My dad was raised by a single mom and they were very close, but he never knew his dad. He went into the army at an early age because he was getting into trouble around the neighborhood.

When I lived with him, I got close to his girlfriend and spent most of my time with her. When she worked nights, then I tried to spend my time around my grandparents because I just wasn't comfortable around my dad.

Then one night, he molested me.

He waited for his girlfriend to go to work and for my grandparents to go to bed upstairs before he started drinking. He was upset with his girlfriend over an argument they had earlier that day. They didn't have the best relationship because my dad would always be accusing her of cheating on him or spending too much money.

After my mom had left him in San Francisco, he became bitter, angry, controlling and insecure. His insecurity had now even accelerated because his girlfriend was 20 years younger than him. So, his drinking grew worse.

On this particular night, I wasn't feeling well so I went to bed early. I had turned my light off in an attempt to rest, hoping I would feel better. When he came in, he did not turn on the light. He just stood by the door for a few minutes. The scent of alcohol filled the room, so I got nervous.

After a few moments, he asked me what was wrong. I told him I was not feeling well. He said, "Let me rub some ointment on your chest." I replied that I was fine and that I just needed to rest. He said I would feel better if he rubbed my chest. I did not want to argue with him because I knew he was already mad at his girlfriend, so I said okay.

He unbuttoned my top and as he was putting ointment on my chest, he took his time massaging me as if he was enjoying it. Then, he started rubbing my breast, my tummy and then down my legs. Suddenly, he moved his hands and started rubbing inside my thighs.

I told him "I am fine! That's enough Dad!" He ignored me and kept rubbing. Then he took advantage of me. I was frozen and in total shock! I did not understand why my own dad would touch his very own daughter so inappropriately.

I cried for days, but I didn't tell anyone because I was too embarrassed. "Why Lord? This is my father! I thought he loved me!" My dad knew how abusive Mom was to me and how much I suffered, but instead of him protecting me, helping me get past it, he took total advantage of me which added more pain to the abuse.

From that moment on, I began to shut down, showing no emotions. I became numb to everything around me, even more than I had been before. I didn't know who to tell or who to trust, so I kept to myself.

I was just going through the motions every day, feeling numb. It got so bad, I just shut down and told my dad, "I want to go back home to mom." My dad showed no remorse for what he did to me and it continued with my other sisters when they moved in with him.

In my later years, I tried to get answers from him, but he couldn't explain it. He just said it was the liquor. Soon, I was living with my mom again. Nothing had changed except all my other sisters had moved out.

I stayed at home with my mom because I did not know what else to do. I was not ready to be on my own. I was vulnerable and confused about myself, so I figured I'd rather stay with my mom and be physically abused than stay with my dad and be sexually violated. Those were my only choices. **I questioned God, "Why did you put us** with bad parents? What did we do to deserve this abuse?"

Chapter 7

Pregnant, Wild, Unstable & Naive

As time went on, I created a fantasy world for myself to block out my pain and hurt. I would pretend I was pregnant; wear big clothes and walk around with my stomach pushed out like I was five months pregnant. I thought if I got pregnant, I would have someone to love me.

It eventually happened because I started seeing the guy next door. He was a lot older than me, but I liked him anyway. I would climb out of my bedroom window at night after my mom went to sleep. I went to him because he gave me what I wasn't getting at home: Attention.

My excitement at home was watering the grass and coloring rocks that I collected off the street, which I used as my imaginary family.

My relationship with the guy next door lasted for a few months. My mom found out what I was doing so she locked the window and I had to go to the front door and knock to get in. She met me at the door and I got beaten for going over to his house. When I got away from her, I ran to my sister's house, but I eventually went back. I was a sheltered child so I did not feel I had enough street sense to leave for good and be on my own.

I found out a short while later that I was pregnant. Then my mom found out and she tried to beat my baby out of me. I ran away again to my dad's house. I only stayed with him for a few weeks because my mom convinced me to come back home. She was a little different with me when I came back home, in a good way. She took me to my doctor appointments, bought the proper foods for me to eat and took me shopping for baby clothes.

I had a baby boy and once I had him, things got better between me and my mom. I guess having a grandchild around softened her heart. Things were really great for a few years with me because my baby kept me busy. My relationship with my son's dad was okay, not the best. Nevertheless, we moved into an apartment together and I got a job right away. I was so excited because I now had my own family that loved me.

Things were good with us for a few months, but suddenly, I found myself taking care of both my son and his dad. I felt as if I was still a child myself as he became possessive and emotionally abusive. I soon discovered that he really didn't love me. I was just his meal ticket!

One day while he was at his music rehearsal, my mom and friends came and moved me out. Shortly after, I was feeling empty again. I just longed for something more than what I was getting or doing with myself.

Once again, I was feeling a real deep emptiness within me. I tried to fill the void by partying, hanging out and catching up on things that I had missed out on while growing up. I hung out with my sisters and it took my mind off the emptiness. I just wanted to party and have fun, so I did.

It was a fun time for me and I was feeling good about my life as an independent young woman. I had my apartment again, my first job and a car. I felt real good about where I was in life because I blocked the past out. Even though I felt good about myself, I still didn't know how to speak up.

When I moved into my second apartment, two of my sisters moved in with me. Then my nephew and his girlfriend came in and took over, eating up all the food, keeping the lights on all night and playing loud music. I didn't say anything because I didn't want to live by myself or lose my sisters like I lost my parents back in San Francisco when they separated. So as a result, I stayed in my room and kept my mouth closed.

The partying continued for a few years, then finally they moved on. Once again, I felt alone and abandoned.

Chapter 8

Who Am I?

I now have two children by myself, being a wild child. I felt I was going nowhere fast, just existing. Eventually things began to change and being a mother became more important to me. I felt different, like I was growing up and maturing. I stopped partying as much and started focusing on my children, but I was still trying to fill a great void inside of me.

Throughout my life for 30 years, I struggled with holding that secret in which also effected my relationships with men. I had "trust" issues, so I never felt safe enough to completely open up to a man. I felt they would just use it against me.

I found myself struggling in and out of different relationships that never lasted too long, but here I am with my third child. I always had my wall up because I always felt I needed to protect my heart and feelings, so I did. That way I didn't have to worry about someone hurting me or leaving me. I kept my wall up a lot. I thought after I had my children and married I would feel secure and loved. I thought the void of feeling empty would go away. It did for awhile, but then I started to long again for that void to be filled. It was like a roller coaster. I could not shake it. The emptiness of not having someone to love me, kept my heart unsettled.

I still felt there was something more missing in my life. I didn't feel complete It was like the feeling I had with my first child; I was so excited, but after a while the excitement wore off. I was feeling unfulfilled, like a piece of me was missing.

One day I was watching television, playing with the channels and I landed on a Christian station, TBN. Not having a relationship with God, not even sure if I had a desire, I found myself enjoying the program. I felt some type of connection when I watched the show.

I was skeptical because of my past experience with Islam. I knew I did not want to be around angry people that preached negativity or reminded me of my childhood, so I didn't watch the Christian program too often, but when I did, I enjoyed it.

In the meantime, I found myself chasing love, trying to fill a void once a gain. I cut my hair short and changed the color to blonde. I got a body makeover, liposuction, tummy tuck. I did all kind of things to make myself feel better about who I was, but nothing I did would fix me. I found myself in the music industry around people looking to get over my pain but that didn't do it. I even found myself buying properties, buying cars and making a lot of money and still that didn't help me feel better.

Even during marriage, I thought, "Well if I get married, I would have someone to love me." We stayed married for ten years and that didn't work out. Things were getting really bad for me. As a married woman, I was living the single life because I wasn't happy. I was out of control. I knew it, but no one held me accountable for my behavior. I was very promiscuous because my husband couldn't give me what I needed. We separated first then later we got a divorce.

I desperately needed Jesus because I messed up, but I was clueless. There was something much deeper I was searching for, but I couldn't find it. I couldn't put my hands on it. Nothing, nothing I did filled the hole in my heart. I was just yearning for something bigger and greater, but I didn't know where to go or how to find it.

I remember I thought if I made myself look beautiful and got a makeover then I would find the right person to love me. The outer beauty wasn't the problem, I needed healing on the inside. I was just hurting so much on the inside, trying to find a way to fix it because I was out of control. I was looking for love in all the wrong places feeling hopeless. God knew what I needed and I was slowly drawing closer to God.

Each struggle I went through drew me closer to God. God was letting me know that's not what you need. He was preparing me for greater blessings to come. Remember, on the other side of adversity is a gift from God.

I began to notice the little things that brought me peace like some quiet time to myself watching TBN or when I didn't have a lot to do and I could just sit and enjoy the moment. I started feeling the Lord's presence around me.

Chapter 9

Deep Soul Searching And Self Evaluation

After my husband and I separated, I felt uneasy about all the stuff I had. It was not making me happy. It was not easy for me to clean house and get rid of all the clutter in my life. I was on overload, trying to manage everything by myself which was too much for me to handle. I downsized everything I owned.

My 2300 square foot home, income properties, luxury cars, expensive jewelry, clothes and furniture. I walked away from most of the stuff and I sold the rest. I moved out of my home into a 600 square foot condo so I could be free to connect and draw close to God. I felt at peace through the situation and felt freedom. That was the beginning of my search for a spiritual connection with God. I wanted peace and fulfillment.

I felt God planned my steps once again. It took a few years to just soul search, change my thinking, change my environment, work on myself, read some self-help books and start reading the Bible. I became more spiritually connected with God.

A year passed, I started feeling even better about myself. I felt I had my peace and I had a connection even though I wasn't going to church regularly. I did something every day to connect with God. I listened to the Gospel music, sermons, surrounded myself with positive people and made a conscious effort to say good things about myself everyday. I was building my relationship with God and feeling really good about where I was spiritually. Once again, God planned my steps. He knew I was longing for love, but I had to be prepared to receive it.

The day God blessed me with a man to love me rightly, I was ready. He was so loving and genuine. He just loved me. He loved me and I felt love. I felt love and it was great! We were in love and together for a little while before I found out I had cancer.

Chapter 10

Cancer And My Journey With God

All God's planning and His divine connection had begun preparing me in so many ways for that dark unforeseen day that would turn my life upside down. Divine order was God's plan. I was in a place of peace and comfort, ready to take on the world because of the relationship I had with God and the wonderful man in my life. I don't think I would have been able to get through the cancer if God had not planned my steps.

I thank God for preparing me at the right time for what I was about to go through. Prior to falling, I called my doctor because I noticed a lot of changes in my knees and my stomach. My stomach used to be flat so I knew something was wrong. My body started taking a turn for the worse. I felt myself going to the doctor complaining about my stomach blowing up and my knees swelling.

My doctor didn't think much about it. She thought maybe there was water building up on my knees. But I was constipated a lot, which was highly unusual. Let me say "We need to be more proactive and listen to our instincts." God was telling me something so I continued to tell the doctor I felt something was wrong, but she insisted that nothing was wrong and I believed her. She's the doctor, so I listened.

She gave me some medicine for the constipation and told me to elevate my legs, so I did. The day came and it happened one early morning. I was at the Laundromat, washing my clothes. I finished washing, had my clothes in a basket and I was walking down the street to my car when I tripped and fell because of a crack of the sidewalk. There were three men close by who helped me up. I thought I had twisted my ankle or pulled a hamstring. I told myself that I was fine.

The three men offered to give me their numbers just in case I was going to have a lawsuit, but I felt fine. A little sore and my ankle was a little tender, but I didn't think much of it.

Within the next couple of weeks, I just thought, it's just a hamstring and it's going to get better. All the while I had my loving guy right there beside me. But, the injury started getting worse. I was having more pain in my right thigh, but I still didn't think it was anything serious. I just tried to stay off of it by elevating my legs.

One particular day, I felt this pain shoot up my right leg and it was very excruciating. I called my doctor again because the pain got worse. I went in and she looked at my injury and ordered x-rays. I got the x-ray, then I was sent to see an orthopedic doctor. He focused on my knee so he didn't notice anything unusual. He told me to go home, get on a life cycle and exercise for 15 minutes. That made the pain worse. I felt God was guiding me through the whole situation because I knew in my heart something was wrong. Unfortunately, the pain got even worse.

I went to the hospital again, emergency x-rays were done and the discovery was obvious; there was a huge hole in my right leg, the size of my hand. I had emergency surgery and they found out I had cancer (multiple myeloma). All the while God was sending me through this in preparation of His plan for me. I felt I had developed a really good relationship with God. I was walking with Him, so I felt good about where I was. I felt very peaceful knowing He was carrying me through this.

When the orthopedic doctor came in my room, he said, "I'm sorry, Ms. Williams, you have cancer." He began to describe in detail what I had and how it was going to affect me, which I thought was unprofessional. Mind you, he was an orthopedic doctor (a bone specialist). He said, "You have multiple myeloma, it's a blood disease. It's going to affect your whole body and take over."

Without saying a word, I just continued looking at him trying to break me. He said, "I'm sorry for what you're going through. I hope you have family with you and a lot of support because you're going to need it."

Well, I had this look on my face, a peaceful look. I knew it was the Holy Spirit in me. It's not that I didn't care or that I wasn't concerned. I understood my pain was legitimate, but suffering from time to time is part of human condition as we go through at some point in our life. So it didn't affect me in a devastating way.

I listened to him and I said to him, "You know, this is the Lord's temple and He can have His way with me." He said, with a smirk on his face, " Did you hear what I said?" And I said, "Did you hear what I said? You need Jesus." He just dropped his head and walked away.

At that moment, I felt victorious because I knew I was a conqueror and the devil had no control over me. Despite what I just heard, the devil wasn't going to win. I was feeling good just knowing God was in my life and I wasn't going through this alone. I'll say it again, "Be proactive when it comes to your health."

The doctors don't know you like you know yourself. You know when something is wrong. God has given us good sense to know when something is not right, so listen. The doctors only know what you tell them and unless you push to take action to get results, they won't do much because they're not in the business of more acceptable care, so be proactive when it comes to your health.

After the doctor told me I had cancer, for some reason, I felt a sense of peace come over me. It wasn't that I wasn't concerned about myself, but I knew the Lord was taking care of me. Knowing my body was the Lord's temple, I knew I would get through this. I didn't dwell on it, I didn't give it a whole lot of thought about what I was going to go through. I just knew God had strengthened me and prepared me for this moment as I was building my relationship with Him.

I embraced it with a positive attitude even knowing what I was going to go through. The thought of going through radiation, losing my hair from chemotherapy, physical therapy to walk again, weight gain from steroids and being labeled "disabled," I knew, but I just didn't let it consume me.

All that I was about to go through was not as hard as having my faith tested right now by God. This was a big test of my faithfulness. I've had my moments where I had doubts about my faith. I struggled from time to time questioning myself about the possibility of something going wrong, even wondering if I should have a Plan B because I had not been walking with God for long. I wasn't going to church to worship, so I thought maybe God would consider that factor, but that was just the devil speaking to my mind, trying to break my faith. God said, "Trust in me with just a mustard seed of faith" and I did. I turned it over to God and started dealing with it one day at a time, feeling peaceful through reading the scriptures and listening to the Gospel.

I quoted many verses of scripture out loud. "I can do all things through Christ who strengthens me," Philippians 4:13. "Greater is He who is in me than he who is of this world," 1 John 4:4. "Trust in the lord with all your heart. Do not depend on your own understanding. Seek His will in all you do and He will direct your path," Proverbs 3:5-6. "Be glad for all God is planning for you. Be prayerful and patient in time of troubles," Romans 12:12.

I kept myself armed with God's Word. Each time I spoke the Lord's words, I felt peaceful, very peaceful. It was my faith, my faith that got me through every situation, every moment of pain, every waking night of pain. It was God's Word alone that kept me going one day at a time.

I kept reciting Philippians 4:6, "Do not be anxious about anything, but in every situation, by prayer and supplication with thanksgiving, presenting your requests to God and ask Him to help you to know what He is doing in you." I kept thinking and mediating on His Word for peace, strength and healing.

I was in the hospital for about a week. When I got out, I was in a wheelchair because I had a 22 inch rod in my right leg and I could not walk. I had a lot of pain medicine to help control the pain in my leg. It took about a month before I got with an oncologist to put together a plan to fight the cancer.

Chapter 11

The Real Healing Power Of God In My Life

During that period, I had sleepless nights, help around the clock to make sure my needs were met throughout the day. I had this wonderful man in my life and my family working together.

It's amazing how God works His plan in us for His purpose even when we are prideful and won't give in. Prior to my situation, my family became very distant after our parents died. Everybody just went their own separate ways. When this happened to me, all my family came from different states to my house and embraced me with a lot of love. I noticed that every difference we had that kept us apart was no longer important.

I saw it as a very joyful, loving and peaceful moment that was long overdue. God knows His children. He knows our faults so he has to use extreme measures to break that negative spirit we try to hold on to sometimes. I thank God for doing that because I missed my family. It was so wonderful to have all my family at home with me. It had been several years since we had all gotten together. God made it happen. Thank you, Lord!

Everything that was going on in my life kept a smile on my face and I just felt blessed and loved. Not to forget about my niece Colleen who was very supportive and patient from day one, taking me to the doctor everyday. God has a way of working things out even if we don't understand. He took a negative situation and turned it into a positive blessing for me and my family. I give God the glory because He is so awesome! This is also His way of maturing His children.

When my bones would ache so bad, I would cry myself to sleep by just singing praises and saying, "By the blood of Jesus, I am healed" over and over again.

God's words were the only thing that gave me comfort and peace in my most difficult time. I knew if I allowed my situation to paralyze me, I would miss my blessings. We can't understand when God wants to use us to make a way for other people. Just trust and obey, knowing He always thinks larger than we do. I just said, "Lord use me as I stay focused and pray."

Chapter 12

The Greater The Challenge, The Greater The Grace

Finally, I saw my oncologist. We got together and put a plan in place to treat the cancer. My whole life was turned upside down. It was a full time job going to the doctor two times a week, chemo three times a week and blood work once a week. I was drained, but hopeful.

When God chooses you for His purpose to touch and transform lives, your pain and suffering will be a blessing. Unless you experience the Holy Spirit, you won't know the joy He brings. In spite of what I was going through, the enemy thought he was going to break me, but he couldn't. I kept smiling with a positive attitude, giving God the glory.

I didn't allow my heart to be troubled. John 14:1, "Let not your heart be troubled. You believe in God, believe also in me." I never asked God "Why?" I just told God, "Help me to know what you're doing in me."

Now it's time for my radiation treatment. I had a body makeover some years prior so I was conscious of the way I looked. During the radiation process, I had to be visibly marked all over my body with a permanent marker for the radiation to be effective. I felt disfigured and embarrassed to be in public. It took me a minute to realize God does not define me by the earthly looks of my body or flesh. He defines me by my spirit.

So, I embraced it and found a way to cover the marks with my clothes. I got through the radiation and still had a cuteness working for me. After the radiation, I started the chemo treatment. The chemo consisted of four different medications, two orally with a steroid and two intravenous, which made me a bit nervous. You never know if your body is going to accept or reject that medicine.

So, it became a waiting game, or a trial and error situation. I was on the chemo for eight months. During that period, I gained seventy pounds from the steroids, not food. I could not sleep and I felt so weird. I would be up all night in the backyard, cleaning out my flower beds in a wheelchair. Matter of fact, the hospital gave me a go-go electric wheelchair to get around in which was very cute, so I still had my cuteness.

My fiancée' did his best to stay up with me. He didn't always understand what I was going through so I would get upset with him when he didn't stay up. Being on steroids, in a wheelchair, overweight and wired was so difficult to handle. My body was drained, but my mind would not shut down and give me a break. I was exhausted.

After being on the medicine for eight months I started feeling really sick. This was another sign something was going wrong and my body was shutting down. I was walking around like a zombie with a fever. I was very cold even when it was hot. I had layers of clothing on when I went to pick up my daughter from school. She kissed me and said, "Mommy, you're really hot." I didn't think much of it, but when I got home, I was feeling very cold, so I called my doctor and told him what was going on. He told me to get to the hospital right away because my temperature was 104.

They ran tests and found out I had a mass lesion in my buttocks. I thank God for the warning signs telling me something was wrong. You don't always know when something is happening, but just know, it's happening for a reason. God was telling me something was happening with my body. Once I found out I had the mass lesion in my buttock, It meant the medicine wasn't working any more. So once again, I'm going to be taking something different to see if it will be effective. I had personally thought that medicine was a "one size fits all" scenario, but discovered that's not true.

The Lord is always on time and He says, "You live by your faith in what you believe, what you know to be true, not by what you see or hear or feel." I was in the hospital for a few days, then I got with my doctor and I started on a different medicine, which was much stronger. Once again, it became a trial and error situation to see if the medicine was going to work.

I was on the medication for maybe four months before I noticed some changes in my face. Around my mouth and my forehead, it was darker than the rest of my face. My hands and feet were turning dark also. My feet looked like an alligator's feet. It was very hard for me to stand because I felt like I was walking on rocks. My feet were very tender and swollen. The doctor said, "Give your body a chance to get used to the medicine, then you will feel better."

One day I was on the computer looking up my medicine and the side effects. What I read was that the medicine can make you worse and it did! I found out I had neuropathy which is nerve damage. I had it in my legs and hands. It messed up the nerves in my legs so bad I could hardly walk. I spoke with my doctor about it and he tried to sugar coat it by saying, "Regardless of that, it's helping the pain." I said, "No, it makes me worse." I felt God was saying, "Don't take it!" So I immediately stopped taking the medication and I started feeling better.

I also found out that neuropathy can be reversed over a period of time. While I was still recovering, I felt empowered, like I was in control despite the situation because I had the Lord with me.

The Holy Spirit was so strong, He would alert me when something was wrong or I needed to consider something else. When the doctors would contradict themselves, I was aware. It would just come to me. I knew it was God. I would say, "This is the Lord. No way is this me." And I would never break down. I had the power, not the doctors. When something wasn't right, I would let the doctor know right away, "This is what I noticed."

I always had a positive attitude. I remember my doctor saying to me, "95% of your healing is attitude. You have a good attitude and you're handling your situation very well. You're going to be just fine." I knew right there, God was speaking to me through him. I was going to get through this illness, and I was going to be even better than I was before.

I started feeling like a guinea pig because I had been on different medicines and now the new medication wasn't working either. I felt as if I was being used to test different medicines and procedures out just to determine their effectiveness. So, I finally told my doctor, "You have to come up with something better. I'm not taking any more medicine. Look at what it's doing to me."

I knew God had another plan for me. I kept saying, "Greater is He who is in me than he who is in the world." That was my statement of faith which was embedded in my heart. I knew I was a child of God and that whatever I was going through, I was going to go through it. "This too shall pass," is what I kept shouting. I kept declaring, "Faith is the substance of things we hope for will happen."

Knowing that, I found strength and hope throughout my journey. I believed that God allowed everything to happen for a reason. It was his voice speaking to me, as it says in Hebrews 11:1, "Now faith is confidence in what we hope will happen and assurance about what we do not see."

After talking with my doctor I said, "Seriously Doctor, it's time to come up with a better plan. No more playing with me!" He said to me, "You know, you don't have any other problems with your body. You just have the cancer. You're a great candidate for a transplant which is a stem cell transplant." Knowing my trust was in God, I knew this was His plan. So, I told the doctor, "Tell me about it then so I can do some research and get back with you in a week."

Within a few days, I decided to go with the plan to have the stem cell transplant done. I was positive this was God's plan for me. When you can't hear his voice, just trust, knowing on the other side is a blessing waiting. So, I trusted God with all my heart.

So, I began to prepare for the transplant which took about two months of preparation. I had to go through the process of getting the cells to come out of my bones so I could go in the hospital to have the transplant. The part about getting the cells to come out of my bones was the hardest part of the process. I had to give myself two shots daily in different areas of my body; my arms one day, the next day in my stomach, then the third day in my thighs for two months straight.

During that time, my body became very stiff and contracted after the first week of the shots. The pain was so unbearable I couldn't sleep. When the cells were coming out of my bones it felt like I was being pulled in two different directions, like a tug of war. The pain was excruciating. I needed assistance with everything around the clock. I couldn't sleep, my stomach went from constipation to diarrhea. My body was taking a major beating. I could hardly bear the pain, but I had to keep going and not stress myself. So, again, I learned to take it one day at a time, thanking God for another day.

Before I went to the hospital for my transplant, I met another woman that also had multiple myeloma in her back. She was so worried about going through the transplant. She was so upset and stressed to the point that her surgery had to be postponed. God worked it out this way. He made it possible for me to go before her and have my transplant. Then when I was done, I was able to walk her through the whole process. I helped ease her mind and her transplant was also successful. I thank God for using me to help her. Colossians 3:16, "Let the message about Christ, in all it's richness, fill your lives. Teach and counsel each other with all the wisdom He gives."

During my time in the hospital for my transplant, I stayed a whole month. My body shut down and I had to be isolated. That was the lowest point in my life because I was cut off from the world, which felt like I was on an island by myself. I kept remembering and reciting scriptures, just to get through it.

John 6:63, "The Spirit gives life, the flesh counts for nothing." I just kept trying to keep a positive attitude knowing that I would get through this. Proverbs 3:5-6, "Trust in the Lord with all your heart, do not depend on your own understanding." James 1:3, "When troubles come your way, let it be an opportunity for joy; for when your faith is tested, your endurance has a chance to grow, so let it grow. For when it is fully developed, you will be stronger in character and ready for anything."

I felt the Lord was building my strength, preparing me for greater things. I would focus on the positive things around me and count my blessings. I loved laughter so I would watch stand up comedy and anything that made me laugh. I also listened to Gospel music to relax me and I spent time in the bible. I realized what I was going through wasn't about me, it was about my purpose.

Colossians 3:2, "Set your mind on things above, not on earthly things." I didn't let the negative thoughts get in my spirit and start saying, "poor me" or "Lord, why are you doing this to me?" Thessalonians 5:18, "Rejoice always, pray continually, give thanks in all circumstances, for this is God's will for you in Christ Jesus." Whenever the doctor would come into my room at the hospital and ask me, "How are you doing, Ms. Williams?" I would say, "I am blessed and highly favored." I wasn't giving the devil any power, despite what I was going through.

During the process of my transplant, I was having an out of body experience to help me cope. I had tubes everywhere, monitoring my every move. The medicines going in from three different IV's were turning flips in my stomach and the morphine given to me only made the pain worse. I kept telling myself, "It's not about me. It's not about me. This is the Lord's work and I'm going to come out of this victorious, for I am more than a conqueror."

I got through it! I overcame the challenge and now because of it, my faith is stronger, wiser and better. I thank God for the opportunity to serve him. I got out of the hospital and I was doing fine.

I was back at home, but now my relationship has taken a turn for the worse. My fiancée' and I were not getting along. He felt I was not able to take care of his needs anymore. He couldn't understand that I needed to heal and not to be overloaded with his requirements or demands.

Once again, God was telling me something. He was planning my steps. I realize people come into your life for a reason, a season or for a lifetime. My fiancée' was in my life for a reason. God put him in my life to fill a void, to love me while I was healing, which he did. The breakup was very painful and I was devastated. I knew it was for the best because once I went into the hospital, he became very insecure about himself and he blamed me.

I cried a lot thinking I just wanted my peace back so I could heal. I wanted the peace back I used to have with God. I remember one day, when I was in church with my fiancée', I cried to the pastor and told him, "I'm so broken. I'm just so broken." I cried out loud shouting, "I want my peace back so I can heal." I need my relationship with Jesus back!" At a point in my life I was going through it with my fiancée', and because of our situation, I had very little time to myself. As a result after I got out of the hospital, I didn't feel that strong connection with God and I wanted that connection back.

God heard me loud and clear. He heard my cry, but He had to plan my fiancée's exit and He did. I cried for three days after he moved out, but it finally hit me when God said, "You asked for your peace and now you got it." When I realized that, I shook it off and I started to move forward and get my joy back!

Chapter 13

God's Key For Breaking Through The Struggles

I continued thanking the Lord every day for my peace, wisdom, knowledge and the understanding of the things that were happening in my life that I didn't understand at the moment. I was so concerned about my fiancée' and I being together despite the unhappiness I was feeling. I couldn't see the bigger picture.

We had moved into this house together, now I began to wonder how I was going to take care of everything alone. "How am I going to take care of myself? How am I going to get through all this stuff by myself? Who is going to help me?"

Then I heard the Lord say, "Haven't I been with you all this time? Haven't I taken care of all your needs?" His words hit me like a ton of bricks. "Yes, Lord, you have," and I started smiling as I thought of Him.

"Thank you, Lord! Thank you for taking care of me and for giving me my peace back." At that very moment, I knew I was okay. It was just the greatest feeling! He gave me that peace that passes all understanding. Philippians 4:7, " The peace of God which transcends all understanding will guard your hearts and minds in Christ Jesus." So now it's me, my daughters and the Lord. I started seeing a greater picture in my life of wanting to do more to make a difference in this world.

I began asking the Lord to enlarge my territory, to direct my path and to tell me, "What do you want me to do with my life now that you saved me?" I knew the Lord had saved me to serve. I knew that was my purpose. I kept searching and praying to God, more and more, for direction. I would spend a lot of time in the Bible to get a deeper and more intimate relationship with Him so I could understand His Word and my purpose.

At first, I thought my purpose was all the gifts, talents and inventions that He had given me. I would say, "Lord, you've given me all these gifts, inventions and talents, now what? What do you want me to do with it? I know you didn't give me these gifts just to sit on it."

I struggled with that though for over a year. I was trying to get my inventions patented and on the market. I was frustrated and upset because nothing would pan out. "Lord, Why?" I said. I learned that your situation will begin to change if you start giving God's Word priority, make prayer a main part of your life and take the focus off yourself.

I soon discovered that God was telling me what He wanted me to do every time He closed a door on a business that I was trying to start up. What's amazing, I kept saying, "God saved me to serve," but I wasn't hearing myself. When you can't hear His voice, learn to just trust His plan. He sees you and He understands. Knowing that on the other side of adversity was a gift waiting for me from God, I just stopped and took the time to listen.

I asked God to give me a divine connection. "Father, I need to be closer to you and with more of my family." Even though my family came out of the woodworks for me, some of them eventually went back to their old ways. I wanted a Christian family and he gave me one. I knew if I had mentors, advisors, counselors and partners, I could get my gifts out. I could get them on the market. There were a few people in my life, but God had another plan.

I was focused more on the gifts He had given me, but not on the bigger picture. I tried not to think about it much for a while. I said, "God has a plan for me and His plan will come together in His time. So, I took my mind off myself and started a family tradition.

During Christmas, I put together a community celebration by inviting all my neighbors, friends and family over to celebrate the birth of Christ. I went around the room with my recorder and asked each person, "What are you thankful for?" I was so excited about this new tradition because it brought people together and helped me take the focus off myself.

When you know that it's not about you and it's about the Lord's work, your real purpose on this earth then becomes more visible. I brought an exchange student into my home from Japan. It was the greatest experience I ever had. To have her in my home, gave me a chance to make a difference in her life. Before Junna left to go back to Japan, she told me I taught her a lot about living a peaceful life. Junna then informed me that she was going home and would learn more about Jesus. She wanted to live a happy and peaceful life like me.

I wasn't aware of everything I was doing, but Junna was taking notes. Junna did a college presentation on my Christian lifestyle. Junna asked me, "Why did you become a Christian?" I told her, "I was unhappy with my life. I felt I didn't have a sense of my purpose and I needed to be fulfilled. Once I received Jesus, I felt alive and fulfilled. I felt completed." She knew at that moment I was speaking from my heart.

My daughter, Kaelin was sitting there at the time. She said, "I didn't know that." I knew God was pleased with me after hearing what I said. I said, "I am what I am, which is a child of God and a citizen of Heaven. I live my life to please God. I am blessed in so many ways to make a difference and touch lives."

God has a plan for all of us. He wants us to prosper but we have to wait on him. He knows our everyday needs. It says in Matthew 6:27, "I know your everyday needs and I will take care of them daily, if you live for me and make the Kingdom your primary concern." I believed that with all my heart.

One day it came to me as I was going into my exchange student's room. If it wasn't for Junna being in my house I wouldn't have found my calling to God's divine order. I happened to go in her room to open her blinds, when I looked over onto her desk and there was this book that caught my eye. I picked it up and read a few pages and I was amazed by the story. A light went on in my head when I read, "People can take and steal your gifts but they can't steal your story. It's your story."

I knew at that moment, that was my calling, that is what God called me to do. Wow! All this time I didn't see it, but I was speaking it. I've been sharing my story with people about my life and how God had saved me through so many difficult situations. How he saved my home, saved my life and healed my broken heart. So many other times, I remember it was time for my three month checkup and my doctor told me the cancer was back after I had the transplant, I said, "The devil is a liar." I was very calm and peaceful when I said it. Joshua 1:9, "Have I not commanded you? Be strong and courageous. Do not be discouraged for the Lord your God will be with you wherever you go." This verse carried me through the battlefield. It was my life verse and my rock.

I wasn't affected by what the doctor said. I said, "What happened? I thought you said the transplant was good for two to seven years." The doctor then said to me, "Nothing is guaranteed." I said, "The Lord is my guarantee!" I walked out of the doctor's office and I never went back. My faith was so strong because I knew God was working something greater and bigger than me and that it was just a matter of time when it would be revealed to me. Until then, I took a six month vacation.

From January to July 2013, I did not see an oncologist or any other doctor during that period. I said, "The Lord is my healer and this is His temple. He healed me and saved me to serve so I will wait on Him." I took my mind off myself.

While I was waiting on God to give me his direction, I took a vacation and I went to Jamaica twice. The first time was for me, then I went back two months later to take clothes to a grandmother of eight that I had met while I was there the first time.

Then I ran a 5K marathon race that I had trained four months for. It was called the "Run for God" marathon and I ran the entire race. It was one of the best feelings ever. I also gave my daughter a big baby shower for her first born. I was busy living and enjoying life and not worrying. I took the focus off myself and just trusted God instead of feeling wounded and looking for pity. Why not look within and be encouraged to find an opportunity to help someone be healed. It's the greatest feeling to give hope to someone.

When it was time for the Lord to give me another doctor, He did. After 6 months, I was led to another doctor, I was tested all over again and there was no cancer. I have a wonderful doctor who works with me and he sees how blessed I am, how peaceful and joyful I am. I'm not letting the doctor tell me what I need to do with my body, I'm letting the Lord lead me. I feel so much better because I have a purpose and it fills me up! I know who I am, because I am a child of God and a citizen of Heaven.

I know how much God loves me because he sacrificed his only Son so I could live for Him and enjoy the fruits of my labor here on Earth. I live purposely to please God, to glorify, honor and to praise Him. I don't have a void in my life anymore. It's been filled with the Holy Spirit. God is so amazing! I cannot describe how peaceful, fearless, bold and courageous I now am. I'm so powerful! I'm confident! I'm loved! I'm whole! I'm living everyday like it's my last day honoring God, sharing the good news about Christ and what I know.

I delight in His name, I wake up peaceful and joyful everyday ready to spread the good news. I'm touching lives all around me and I just love it! It's all because of my relationship with God. Without Him, I am nothing.

I remember when my house was in foreclosure, twenty days from being sold at the auction. I said, "It's time to weather the storm again." I stood still in my living room and I repeated Exodus 14:14, "Be still, I will fight your battles." I also quoted John 15:7, "If you remain in me and my words remain in you, you may ask for anything you want and it will be granted." It was me and the Lord against the world.

When they posted that note on my door, I thought about Colossians 1:16, "God created everything." So I said, "Lord, everything on this earth belongs to you and man cannot take it away." If you want me out of this house then you get me out! But if you want me here, then you, Lord, make a way and save me."

Within two weeks, a real estate friend of mine called to check on me, but that was God. The bank fought with us tooth and nail stating it was too late to submit any modification paperwork. I said, "Send it anyway," and they accepted it. That's just another example of how God has saved me.

There was a time when I was flat broke, I didn't have a dime in my pocket and my mortgage was due. I didn't know how God was going to do it, but I knew in my heart he would take care of me and He did.

I know how much God loves me, He has always come through for me when I needed him. I recognize it more so now that I'm walking with Him.

Proverb 3:5-6, "Trust in the Lord with all your heart, do not depend on your own understanding, seek His will in all you do and He will direct your path." So, stand still and trust despite what you see or think.

Hebrews 11:1 tells us to believe what you want to happen and it will happen as you turn it over to God. Let go and let Him work it out. If you want your situation to get better, then take your mind off yourself and go help someone else. Go sow a seed because what you're saying to God is I trust you, this is your battle, not mine. I need you in my business Lord and only you can handle my situation.

Regardless of its size, God will step right in and take care of the problem. He may not fix it when you want him to, but He's on time all the time. God said, "I will never give you more that you can handle and I will never forsake you." Believe in Him for all his glory, for all his grace, all his mercy, and all his favor. He is awesome!

I think about my life and how good God is. He is taking care of me and my daughter's daily needs. I'm no longer looking for people to provide for me. Matthew 6:25-27, "Don't worry about everyday life – whether you have enough food and drink or enough clothes to wear. Isn't life more than food and clothes? I know your needs, seek the Kingdom of God above all else and live righteously and He will give you everything you need."

Trust God and His Word instead of man's opinion. Don't be fearful or frightened! Stand bold with confidence knowing that the Lord is with you. Look to what you believe, what you know is true! Not what you see, hear or think. Don't trust your own thinking for it bears no fruit. Don't sit around being afraid and wondering where you are going to get your next dollar from or if the cancer is going to come back. I never claimed it, so don't you claim it either.

Don't claim your situation! You may acknowledge its existence, but don't claim it. Don't allow it to consume you! Don't let it get in your spirit. Let the Lord's love fill your spirit and walk in the victory that Christ has given you.

It's not going to always be pretty. If God is going to transform you into what He's called you to do, He has to prepare you for your blessings and miracles. We want our lives fixed without any pain but Jesus suffered for us so what makes us better? Its not going to happen that way. Remember He is sending you through something which means you're going to go through it and then come out victorious.

God allows us to be uncomfortable so He can comfort us and then we can become comforters to one another. Do you know if you don't experience any adversities or challenges, how can you help someone or relate to the situation to be of service? If you have no problems in your life, how boring is that? How are you able to help anyone if you haven't experienced anything? You can sympathize or give a pat on the back, but you can't relate unless you've gone through something.

I went through cancer because God had a purpose for my life so I could make a difference. Ask Him to let you become a light for Him and to touch lives and leave a legacy for His glory. Matthew 5:14-16, "You are the light of the world. In the same way, let your light shine before others that they may see your good deeds and glorify your Father in Heaven." Tell people your story about how much God has done for you and what he's doing for you now. Let the Holy Spirit walk with you each day and build your heart to touch and transform lives.

We can put God aside, thinking we're doing it all on our own; me, myself and I. One day you will serve God because ultimately, it's what we do for others that will count with God in the end, not what we do for ourselves.

I think of it this way, when I signed up for the marathon to run the 5K, I had an expectation to win the race and not just to get a t-shirt to say I participated. The Apostle Paul didn't want to be the guy who just gets the t-shirt, he went for the gold. I too want to win the prize. I want to dominate the race, yank the trophy out of the judges' hand at the finish, to show I am willing to make whatever sacrifices necessary to finish the race, win this fight victoriously and strongly for Jesus.

As a Christian, you've got to make sacrifices for Christ and put in work which makes us partners with Him.

Jesus never told us that after becoming a Christian, our life would get really easy and all our problems would be solved or everything we do will be blessed. He never said it. Jesus said, "If you want to be my disciple, deny yourself and take up your cross and follow me." Count the cost before you come to me because there is one. This isn't easy, comfortable or convenient.

The people that Jesus calls, He calls disciples. He gave the command, "Go into the entire world and make disciples and teach them to observe what I have commanded of you." The word "disciple" comes from the word "discipline."

Discipline is something necessary to become more godly. Some of us work hard to get in shape and we discipline ourselves to stay that way. Try exercising to be more godly because that's more important.

It's not always going to be comfortable and sometimes its going to be really painful. You might think, "I don't want to do it. It's too much of a sacrifice to be a Christian, forget it. If it's painful, then I don't want any part of it." Here's the reality: Life is going to hurt no matter what, but the rewards are great and eternal. Just because it's hard doesn't make it bad.

If living a Christian lifestyle was easy, everyone would be a Christian. Anything worth having is worth fighting for. If you don't stand for something, you'll fall for anything. Sometimes you're suppose to hurt, growing pains are part of your training. Remember there is a prize and a goal in the end. This life is temporary. Life isn't about coasting. There's a prize to living a Christian life the way God tells us to live. It's a prize that will be worth all eternity.

We are all important to God and connected. God created us and his desire is to have a personal relationship with us. You can't control what happens to you, but you can control how you respond to it. Even when you face the worse, do what you can and control your thoughts. Don't give the devil your power. When difficult times come, stir up that hope and belief in the Lord, just knowing that He is with you. He is walking you through your purpose. God will give you the strength to endure the challenges of your heartaches and your pain. Be still and know that the Lord is fighting your battle and know that better days are ahead. For God has a plan for each and every one of us.

Everything good in life begins with hope. Whatever you believe you should never be without. Stay hopeful because hope is where dreams begin along with faith and love. It is the voice of your purpose in life and the pillars of spirituality. It is your push, your step, your blueprint and your guidance. So despite your situation, keep moving ahead. Because as long as you're moving and creating action, you will receive results. You are creating better days for the unexpected opportunities that are coming your way.

Stay hopeful and be challenged, knowing God is building your character, faith and strength. Hold on and trust because sometimes all you have is your belief that anything is possible and that miracles can happen, so just hold on. Walk to the edge and take one more step of faith. The world has so much that can be against us if we live by this world's rule.

Romans 8:31, "If God is for you, who can be against you? How will He not also graciously give us all things?" But if you know the Lord's rule, the Lord's law, then surround yourself with His Word and don't give in to despair. Whatever you're lacking, believe that God will provide and that He will never forsake you.

Leverage your life for someone else, even if they don't deserve it because your life is connected to others. Get comfortable not knowing what's ahead of you and believing what you want to happen will happen through faith. Hebrew 11:1. Take the focus off yourself and let God make your life about something bigger than you. Be passionate about God and people and allow your story to bring healing.

Chapter 14

The Conclusion

I am who I am today, because of what I've gone through, receiving Christ and experiencing the power of God.

Therefore, I humbly encourage you to draw closer to God and live your life to serve like Jesus, so your life will be fruitful. Philippians 1:2-4 reminds us that Jesus lived for the benefit of others and the glory of God. At the end of the day, isn't that all that matters?

Embrace your adversities and sow seeds by spreading the Good News about Christ and bringing people closer to God. People that leave a legacy are leaders whose works will last forever.

Do you want your life to matter? Become a voice for Christ and tell the world about Him. Become a light for Christ and allow your story to make the difference in someone's life. At the end of the day, you want to make sure that your purpose, whatever that looks like, will serve the Lord without distractions.

Ask yourself, "What kind of legacy am I leaving? What would my family and friends say my legacy was and was it fulfilled?" The best basketball player, a successful career, a master's degree or maybe a lot of nice expensive stuff? How about living for the only thing that really matters years from now? That's being a faithful servant for Jesus Christ. Your goals, dreams and stuff are important, but it doesn't matter at the end of the day. There's only a few things in life that are forever.

It's what we do in this life for Jesus Christ that will leave a legacy of love, service and faithfulness. Let God turn you into the person He's calling you to be – a faithful messenger and servant.

I pray that my life can be reflected in Philippians 4:9, "Whatever you have learned or received or heard from me, or seen in me – put it into practice and the God of peace will be with you and continue His work until it is finally finished on the day when Christ Jesus returns.

God bless you on your journey for Jesus Christ.

In Closing...

I remember a time when I was feeling low, I didn't want to share my story. I didn't want to be labeled as handicap. I didn't want to use my parking sticker or the scooter to get around. I was blind-sided by what I thought God wanted me to do. Aside from feeling less than normal or being labeled disabled, I realized the importance of leaving a legacy and making my time on earth count for more than just me, so I took the focus off myself.

My attitude changed as I thought, "There are people with greater challenges than mine." When I viewed it that way, I began to reach out and encourage people to have hope and live with purpose.

Find your purpose! Live out your purpose! Share your story! Because when your story gives hope, your life has meaning and when your life has meaning, you leave a legacy of love, service and faithfulness.

PRAYER

Dear Father in Heaven,

Walk with me each day and build my destiny with your heart to touch and change lives.

Help me to know what you're doing in me so I don't quit on you.

Help me to trust you, when you need me to be an example for other people to believe in you, even when I don't understand.

I know my life can't be perfect or fixed without making sacrifices for you Father, so help me not to allow my disappointment to paralyze me so I can leave a legacy for the people I don't know.

The Future Generations.

A LAST WORD OF ENCOURAGEMENT
FROM THE LORD:

Joshua 1:9 says,

"Be strong and courageous.
Do not be afraid,
For I will be with you
wherever you go!"

PERSONAL ACTION PLAN

Taking a small step daily to build your relationship with God can make a big difference. Read positive materials, listen to gospel and relaxing music and be around positive supporting people.

SCRIPTURE END NOTES

Romans 8:31 – Page 68

"If God is for you, who can be against you? How will he not also graciously give you all things?"

Philippians 4:13 – Page 43

"I can do all things through Christ who strengthens me."

1 John 4:4 – Page 43

"Greater is he who is in me than he who is of this world."

Proverbs 3:5-6 – Page 43

"Trust in the Lord with all your heart. Do not depend on your own understanding. Seek His will in all you do and He will direct your path."

Romans 12:12 – Page 43

"Be glad for all God is planning for you, Be patient and prayerful in times of trouble."

Philippians 4:6 – Page 43

"Don't worry about anything: instead, pray about everything. Tell God what you need, and thank him for all He has done."

Isaiah 53:5

"He was pierced for our rebellion, crushed for our sins, He was whipped so we could be healed."

John 14:1 – Page 47

"Let not your heart be troubled. You believe in God, believe in also in me."

Hebrews 11:1 – Pages 51 and 68

"Faith is the confidence in what we hope for will actually happen; It gives us assurance about things we cannot see."

Colossians 3:16 – page 52

"Let the messages about Christ, in all its richness, fill your lives. Teach and counsel others with all the wisdom He gives."

Thessalonians 5:18 – Page 53

"Rejoice always, pray continually, give thanks in all circumstances, for this is God's will for you in Christ Jesus."

Philippians 4:7 – Page 57

"The peace of God which transcends all understanding will guard your heart and your mind in Christ Jesus."

Matthew 6:27

I know your everyday needs and I will take care of them daily, live for me and make the Kingdom your primary concern."

Joshua 1:9

"Be strong and courageous. Do not be terrified; Do not be discouraged, for the Lord your God will be with you wherever you go."

Exodus 14:14 – Page 62

"Be still. I will fight your battles."

Romans 4:18-22

Even when there was no reason for hope, Abraham kept hoping--believing that he would become the father of many nations. For God had said to him, "That's how many descendants you will have!" And Abraham's faith did not weaken, even though, at about 100 years of age, he figured his body was as good as dead--and so was Sarah's womb. Abraham never wavered in believing God's promise. In fact, his faith grew stronger, and in this he brought glory to God. He was fully convinced that God is able to do whatever he promises. And because of Abraham's faith, God counted him as righteous.

Philippians 3:3 "We put no confidence in human effort."

Matthew 5:14-16 – Page 65

"You are the light of the world. In the same way, let your light shine before others that they may see your good deeds and glorify your father in heaven."

Philippians 4:8

"Finally, brothers and sisters, whatever is true, whatever is noble, whatever is right, whatever is pure, whatever is lovely, whatever is admirable – if anything is excellent or praiseworthy, think about such things and the God of peace will be with you."

INSPIRATIONAL AFFIRMATIONS

God is love.

I will let the sun of life shine on me.

God wants to elevate you. Don't compromise.

I am choosing my future by what I do now.

People don't care what you know until they know you care.

A gift awaits on the other side of adversity.

Worship is my lifestyle.

Embrace adversity. Let it be an opportunity for joy.

If being a Christian was easy, everybody would be one.

Change that proud spirit to a humble spirit.

Live with purpose.

Anything worth having is worth fighting for.

Don't be pitiful, be powerful.

Wait on the Lord, He knows what you need.

Walk like you know who you are.

Your life is shaped by your thoughts.

We become that to which we are committed.

Be firm in faith.

Today I began with the end in mind.

God shaped me to serve.

Do for others on purpose, if you want to get well.

Decide to get well. Part of healing is painful.

I'm taking care of God's business and He's taking care of mine.

Love God with all your heart.

I believe, I receive Jesus Christ as my Lord and Savior.

Be purposely driven for Jesus.

Tell people about Jesus.

Love is time spent.

Be a living sacrifice.

Jesus died so I can live.

God's love is unconditional.

We are citizens of Heaven.

Live obediently.

If you don't stand for something, you'll fall for anything.

I'm a work in progress.

Peacemakers are rare.

God said I qualify.

God has a plan for you.

Learn to love and to relate to others.

God made you to be you.

Only shared experiences can help others. I make my living by giving.

God is shaping me for service.

Be a deep spirited friend.

Attack the problem, not the person.

If you're serving others, you're living.

Talk to God before making a decision.

Begin with sympathy, not solutions.

Your words determine what you will do.

Obedience and sacrifice is a reflection of faith and trust.

God's dead-ends always have a purpose.

God so loved the world, He gave His only son.

God alone is my refuge.

His faithful promises are my armor.

The heart can't embrace what the mind rejects.

My eyes are always looking to the Lord for help.

Give God a blank sheet of paper and let Him fill in the details.

Your circumstances are temporary, but your character will last.

Weather the storm for it builds character.

I'm a servant for God, so I do whatever needs to be done for God.

Despite of the situation, give God the glory.

Simplify your life for Jesus.

Trouble produces patience and patience produces character.

Trouble comes to prove faith is pure.

Remember, God's plan for you is good!

SPECIAL PHOTOS

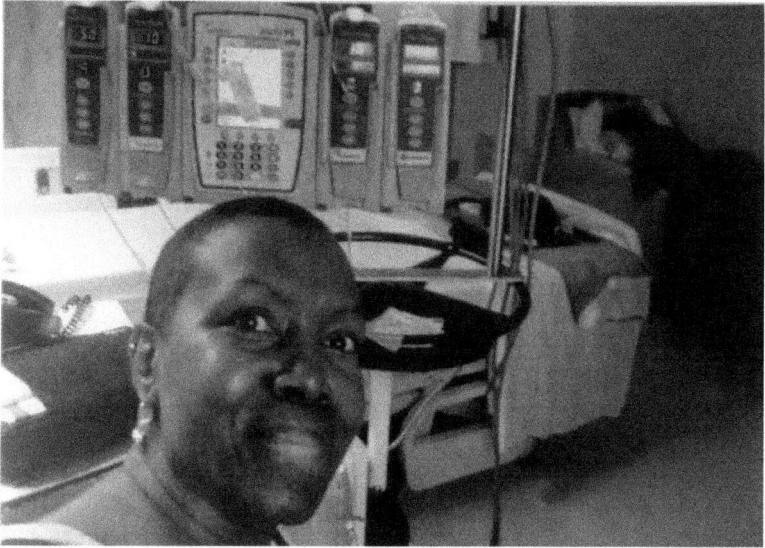

Me at the City Of Hope, having a stem-cell transplant. I kept a smile as I continued to give God all the glory throughout those tough days of my life.

Me at over 200 lbs. I was on chemo and steroids, which took over my body and kept me exhausted.

I went to Montego Bay, Jamaica to help some families after finding out the cancer was back.

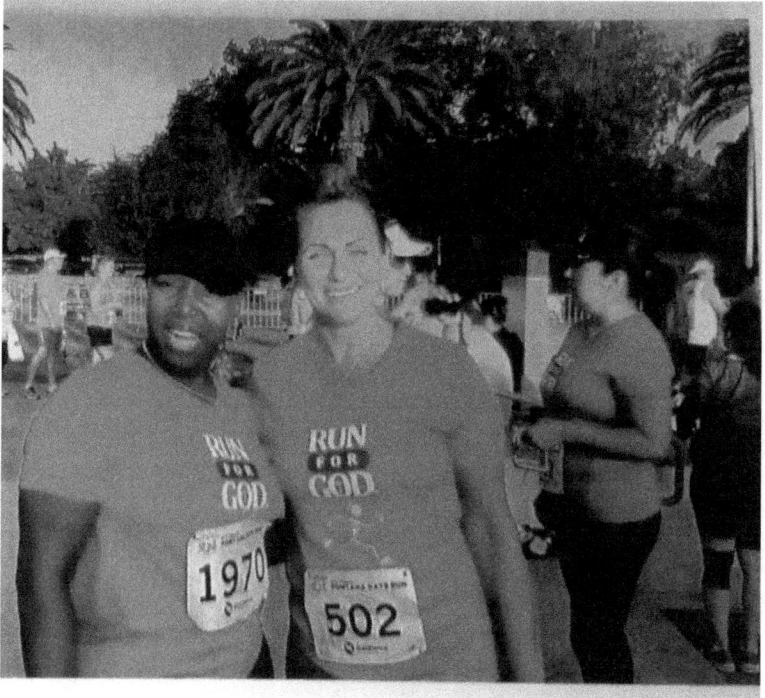

I ran a "Run for God Marathon" after finding out the cancer was back. I took my mind off myself and I kept my focus on God.

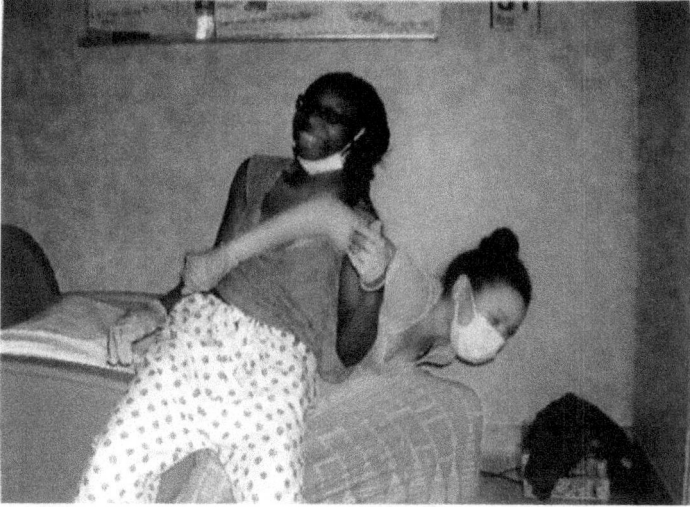

My two daughters, Kaelin and Bre, in my room at City of Hope Hospital playing around cheering me up while I went through my stem cell transplant. I loved it! They kept me smiling.

My mom and her parents

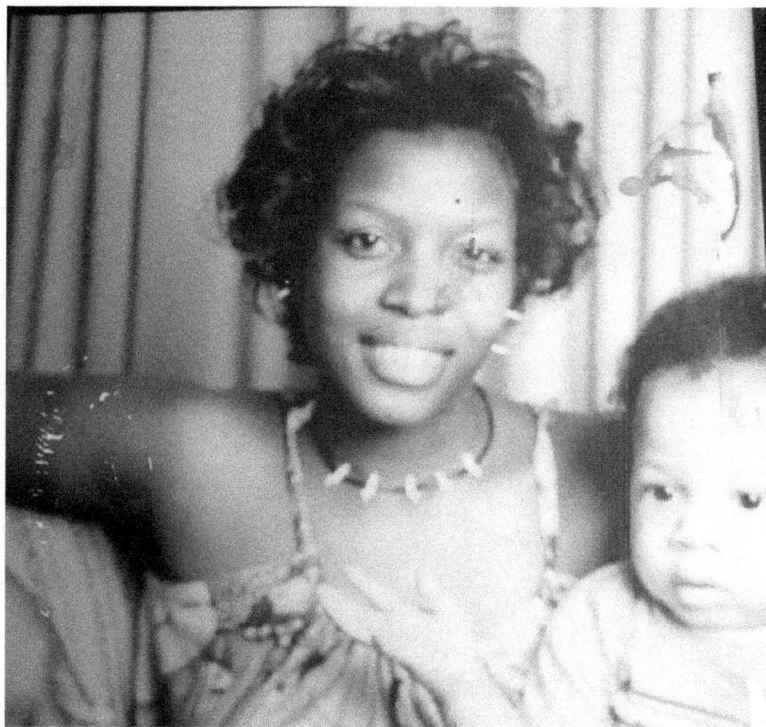

AC with 1st Child

AC WILLIAMS

My dad

My wedding

AC WILLIAMS

My mom Hanna Al-Muquaddim Muhammad as a Muslim,
40 years of service.